New Directions Ministries

P.O. Box 80611
Lansing, MI 48908
Christ Centered Pen Pals

The Presence Of God

DAVE WILLIAMS

The Presence Of God

Of God

*Where Everything
You Could Ever Crave
Or Desire Is Found*

DAVE WILLIAMS

The Presence of God
Where Everything You Could Ever Crave Or Desire Is Found

Unless otherwise noted, Scripture quotations are taken from the HOLY BIBLE, NEW INTERNATIONAL VERSION ®. Copyright © 1973, 1978, 1984 by International Bible Society. Used by permission of Zondervan Publishing House. All rights reserved.

ISBN 0-938020-67-6

Second Printing 2004

Cover Design: Gerard R. Jones

Published by

DECAPOLIS
PUBLISHING
Printed in the United States of America

BOOKS BY DAVE WILLIAMS

Contents

"Everything we need in life is found in the presence of God."

First Word

Several years ago I had a remarkable supernatural experience that changed my life forever.

While in Tulsa, Oklahoma, attending a series of meetings, I decided to visit with my old flight instructor. He was an older man with a gentle manner, and I enjoyed his company greatly. He had flown every type of plane imaginable.

We went to dinner and had a wonderful time. Afterward, we decided to go to his house for coffee, but as I was following him, a car burst into my peripheral vision running a red light and smashing into the side of my rental car. The impact spun my car around in the intersection. When it stopped, I sat for a moment, got my bearings, and examined myself for injuries. Everything seemed fine, but my shoulder was in bad shape. It hurt to touch it, and I could not move it without great pain. As a result, I was taken to the hospital by ambulance. My instructor had not seen the accident and waited at his house, wondering what had happened to me.

After a short stay in the hospital, I went to my hotel to finish out my stay in Tulsa, and that is when the unusual experience happened. Car wrecks and getting bumped and bruised are not so strange; they happen every day to believers and unbelievers alike. But what happened to me while I recovered in that hotel room was very unusual, even for a Pentecostal preacher who believes in the power and presence of the Holy Spirit.

Here is what happened while I lay there alone: *Somebody walked into my room.* This person was not human. He was not visible, and yet He filled the room when He entered it. He was dignified, classy, warm, and attractive.

It was the Holy Spirit.

As I lay there in pain, a smile broke across my face, and I lifted my good arm to praise God, tears rolling down my cheeks and onto the hotel pillow. I felt I was in the Holy of Holies, with God's love bombarding me like the rays of the sun. I wanted to absorb the goodness I felt emanating from Him.

That experience gave me new revelation and changed my view of what matters in the Christian walk. I wish I had experienced two decades earlier what I experienced in that hotel room, because it would have saved me a lot of grief. I learned this simple fact:

Everything we need in life is found in the presence of God.

You can learn about the presence of God, but until you experience it, it remains like a food you know about but never eat, or like a dream that seems real but never comes true. The presence of God is the all-encompassing answer to a question you did not know how to ask. It is the answer to a thousand questions all at once.

The presence of God should be the normal environment for the follower of Christ. Anything less robs us of joy, peace, and all the fullness of the fruit of the Spirit. Everything you could have craved and desired is found in what I am going to share with you.

This book has three simple purposes — to show you how to experience the presence of God, to show you your need for the presence of God, and some of the things His presence will do for you. I pray right now that you will sense the presence of God as you read, when you put the book down, and when you are going about your day. I pray that His Word will dwell richly with you and that you will discover, as I did, this fourth-dimensional relationship with God.

Dave Williams

Chapter 1

Unbreakable Joy

How would you like to come to a place in life where, no matter what happens, nobody could take away your joy? Someone says, "What an ugly dress!" and you just smile. The bank calls and says, "We made an error, and you owe us $5,000," and you are not fazed.

Does that describe you now? Would you like it to describe you?

There is an ingredient, often unknown even to devout Christians, that can make our joy unbreakable. Jesus had it. Do you think He worried that the Pharisees did not like Him? Wanted to trip Him up? Wanted to kill Him? Nothing they did bothered Him. Even when King Herod requested an audience with Him, Jesus could have cared less. "Go tell that fox I am going to continue working miracles and doing

My Father's will," He said, probably to the amazement of His hearers. He was chiefly concerned about remaining in the presence of His Father. He cared what God thought. *That* is the miracle ingredient.

In the presence of the Lord, the Bible says, our enemies perish — enemies such as sin and sickness. Why do some Christians have so many hang-ups, so many problems? Because they are not experiencing the presence of God. Whenever you flee from the presence of God, there is a vacuum, and that vacuum creates all sorts of impostor solutions.

Saints and sinners alike are looking for something or someone to bring joy. We instinctively look to other people, saying, "When I get married, I am going to be happy." Two weeks after the wedding, that ideal disappears. Then follows a litany of other hopes we hang our hats on:

"I will be happy when I have children."

"I will be happy when the children are gone."

"I will be happy when I retire."

When will we learn that none of these things bring lasting joy or happiness? When will we learn that God's presence can bring us genuine and magnificent joy every day of our lives? When we have experienced the presence of God, we do not need other people to encourage us. We do not need affirmation from any other man or woman, not even our spouses!

One Friday I asked my wife, Mary Jo, "How were the services last Sunday?" She said, "They were good." I said, "What did I preach on?" She said, "I can't remember." I did not lose my joy over that, because I had been in the presence of God. I continued, "You do not remember what I preached on Sunday morning?" She said, "No, but you do not remember what I cooked for every meal last week either, and it still fed you!"

She was right. Not often does someone remember a preacher's sermon more than a few weeks, but we all know when we have been spiritually fed. The presence of God stays with us as we abide in Him, and it contains all that we need.

King David discovered this amazing truth. In Psalm 16, he said to God:

> **Thou wilt shew me the path of life: in thy presence *is* fullness of joy; at thy right hand *there are* pleasures evermore.**
>
> **—Psalm 16:11 (KJV)**

In His presence is fullness, or saturation, of joy overflowing to everyone with whom you come into contact. Where is that joy found? In His presence.

Ten seconds in the presence of God can accomplish more than all human effort combined. In the presence of God, our love for Jesus is restored. We rise above life's troubles, and we are no longer satisfied with short-lived strategies and human answers to challenges.

How blessed we are to have His presence! Before Jesus went to the cross and died for the sins of the world, God limited the pervasiveness of His presence in the world. In the Old Testament, the Ark of the Covenant contained the presence of the Lord, and with the Ark came blessings and prosperity. It contained the Ten Commandments, manna, and Aaron's budding rod: things that would remind the Israelites of God's wonderful works.

At one point, the Ark was stolen by the Philistines, and Israel wanted to get it back. So powerful was the presence of the Lord on the Ark that even when it was in the hands of the Philistines, a hard-hearted and stiff-necked people, the Philistines' homes became blessed and prosperous.

David led a group of people to battle; they won and brought the Ark back to Israel.

> (But as the Ark arrived in Jerusalem, David's wife Michal, the daughter of King Saul, felt a deep disgust for David as she watched from the window and saw him dancing like a madman.)
>
> —1 Chronicles 15:29 (TLB)

David was so excited about the presence of God being back in Israel that he danced like a wild man! Michal, his wife, watched with disgust and criticized him for looking like a stooge. The Bible says she remained barren the rest of her life. She represents those who demean the presence of God.

If David was that enthusiastic about the presence of God, what does that say about us? Shouldn't we celebrate it with joy? Shouldn't we show a little emotion? I love the famous little book about a monk, named Brother Lawrence, who practiced the presence of God. It was said that he was always aware of God's presence, as much at prayer as when he was working in the monastery kitchen during busy meal times. He said:

> "I make it my business only to persevere in His holy presence, wherein I keep myself by a simple attention, and a general fond regard to God, which I may call an actual presence of God; a habitual, silent, and secret conversation of the soul with God, which often causes in me joys and raptures inwardly, and sometimes also outwardly, so great that I am forced to use means to moderate them, and prevent their appearance to others."[1]

He became so excited in the presence of God that he forced himself to keep quiet though he probably wanted to jump up and down, dance, twirl, sing, and shout praises!

That is what the presence of God produces in us — unbreakable joy. And there is more! In the next chapter we will see four distinct things the Bible promises us when we remain in God's presence.

Chapter 2

What The Presence Of God Gives Us

In one of his letters, Brother Lawrence wrote, "If I were a preacher, I would preach nothing but practicing the presence of God." *(The Practice of the Presence of God, Conversations and Letters of Brother Lawrence.)*[1]

I feel that way also. If there was one thing I could impart to you as a reader, it would be the magnificence of God's presence — and its availability to you right now.

I am a big fan of roller coasters. About two hours from my home is an amusement park with rides such as the Magnum, the Raptor, the Mean Streak, the Gemini, and the Blue Streak. The problem is, they cannot build a roller coaster big enough, scary enough, or loopy enough for me, because the thrill always wears off. After three or four times, I know what to expect. But the thrill of being in God's presence never wears off.

I am sure that if we tried to count the benefits of being in the presence of God, we would never finish the list, but in 1 Chronicles, chapter 16, we find four specific promises that apply to you and me.

David and the Israelites were bringing the Ark back to Jerusalem in what can only be described as a loud, boisterous, joyful parade led by the dancing king himself. (This was when David's wife scorned him.) David appointed certain people in the procession to do nothing but thank the Lord, appointed others to do nothing but praise the Lord, and appointed yet others to do nothing but record what the Lord was doing.

The Bible records David's song of thanksgiving, and in verse 27 it speaks of God's presence.

> **Splendor and majesty are before Him; strength and joy in his dwelling place. Ascribe to the LORD, O family of nations, ascribe to the LORD glory and strength, ascribe to the LORD the glory due his name...**
>
> **—1 Chronicles 16:27-29a**

Number One: Glory

The first thing that comes to you in the presence of the Lord is glory. Now, this is not the "Shekinah" glory that God will share with no man. This is a different word in the Hebrew language, and it means beauty. Real beauty is found in the presence of the Lord, and no matter how much a person creams her face, grooms his hair, puts bonding or bleach on her teeth, if he or she is not walking in the presence of the Lord, that beauty is merely a shadow.

When I met Mary Jo, there was a radiance about her that drew my attention immediately. She glowed, luminesced, beamed. That is what glory means: beauty, excellence, grandeur, magnificence, brilliance, and importance.

Moses experienced this glow of glory, and the people were frightened to look at him.

> But if the ministration of death, written *and* engraven in stones, was glorious, so that the children of Israel could not stedfastly behold the face of Moses for the glory of his countenance; which *glory* was to be done away:
>
> —2 Corinthians 3:7 (KJV)

Jesus was filled with God's glory all the time, and particularly during the transfiguration when His garments glowed like lightning.

> And after six days Jesus taketh Peter, James, and John his brother, and bringeth them up into an high mountain apart,

> And was transfigured before them: and his face did shine as the sun, and his raiment was white as the light.
>
> —Matthew 17:1-2 (KJV)

Disciples like Stephen were touched with God's glory. When Stephen was martyred, his face glowed like an angel's.

> All who were sitting in the Sanhedrin looked intently at Stephen, and they saw that his face was like the face of an angel.
>
> —Acts 6:15

As people who walk with God, we should "glow" with God's glory. I don't believe glory is limited to the sanctuary or prayer closet, though we can experience unique times of glory as a corporate body or alone in prayer. But glory should billow around us like an invisible cloud everywhere we go — the bus stop, the grocery store, school, and home. People should notice something unusual about us — a warm welcoming atmosphere that only comes from being in God's presence.

Number Two: Honor

Honor means to be esteemed, valued, admired, looked up to, appreciated, desired, and preferred.

Doesn't it feel wonderful to be honored? Don't you feel great when someone appreciates, admires, and looks up to you, or when a fellow Christian treats you with dignity and value?

One of the most critical needs in a person's life is to feel important to somebody. There is not a wife who does not want to be valued by her husband, or a husband who does not want to be admired by his wife. Every dad wants his son or daughter to look up to him. Every mom wants her child to look up to her. Every teacher wants his or her students to look up to him or her. We all want a sense of value, a sense of worth.

- Some people brag to feel important.

- Some people do dangerous things to gain the honor of friends.

- Some people pretend to be sick to draw attention to themselves.

The need for honor, value, and worth is pervasive. Our music minister suffered a loss a recently when his brother walked into his front yard and was shot and killed. The killer took the brother's driver's license before the getaway car sped off. Why? Because you can only gain honor in some gangs if you kill an innocent victim, take his driver's license to the gang leader, and when the gang leader sees the obituary in the newspaper, the murderer is allowed to join the gang.

That is an extreme example of what people will do to gain honor, but in some sense we all perform that way. As much as we draw on other people to fulfill our sense of honor, we will never get enough *except* in the presence of God.

When we are in the presence of God, we attract honor from others. Have you noticed how people defer to men and women of God? When a man carrying the presence of God walks into the room, people are drawn to him. They want to serve him, listen to him, and be with him so that God's presence rubs off on their lives.

Jesus drew great crowds, and people spontaneously honored Him with gifts, praise, and adoration. I love the passage in Mark 9 that tells us that when He came down from the mountain after the transfiguration, people saw Him from a distance and were struck with awe and amazement — simply by looking at Him! It says they immediately ran to greet Him. He had done nothing to draw attention to Himself — no miracles, no preaching at that moment — but the presence of God was obviously with Him, and it drew people like a high-powered magnet.

Christ still draws crowds — through us! The presence of God invites honor from people as they are drawn to the presence of Christ, who lives in us.

I believe that having God's presence in your life will cause people to treat you better at the bank, the store, and at work. You will receive honor from people you do not know because they recognize the nobility of the King who lives inside of you.

• Acquaintances will ask your advice, or seek counsel in difficult situations because they know you have access to supernatural wisdom.

• Your children will respect and obey you as they see you walking with God. They will not know why, but you will seem to have a quiet authority. They will admire you for bringing stability to their lives, and as they become adults, they will honor your example.

• Co-workers and employers or employees will honor you for bringing a presence into the office that has nothing to do with alcohol, pornography, gossip, or foul language.

Honor is a wonderful reward for being in God's presence. You will never feel more admired than when your life is saturated in it.

Number Three: Strength

This word means security, power, might, protection, safeguarding, and immunity. The Bible says:

> A thousand may fall at your side, ten thousand
> at your right hand, but it will not come near you.
>
> —Psalm 91:7

Everyone is looking for security. I read an article about many baby boomers mortgaging their houses to buy into the stock market because they are afraid that there will be no Social Security for them when they retire. Stockmarket security, they believe, is worth the risk.

I knew a lady who left her husband and married a millionaire because she wanted financial security.

We look for strength and security in retirement portfolios, 401(k)s, possessions, power, and reputation. All of these fall short if we do not find security in God's presence.

Let me show you how it works.

After a stressful day of work, taking the kids to piano lessons, then trying to have a few quiet moments with your spouse, you finally walk into your bedroom and hear your soul begging for a few moments with the Lord. You step into your walk-in closet, sit on the stool you normally use for putting on your shoes, and you begin to pray, silently, with whispered words, and silently again. The world around you recedes like watercolors spiraling down a drain; the stress melts away as if it were made of butter. The pressure of the day falls away like booster rockets dropping off a space shuttle as it enters orbit, and soon you are airborne, your soul floating in the serenity, strength, and assurance of God's presence.

He is with you. Nothing else matters. The troubles of the day seem small and insignificant, the obligations easy. You have centered yourself on God, and He is unshakable.

You walked into the closet frazzled and emotionally volatile; you walk out strong and secure, no matter what happens. People sense in you a strength that cannot be taken away by external events. David said:

> **He alone is my rock and my salvation; my fortress, I will never be shaken.**
>
> **—Psalm 62:2**

Security also means receiving the Lord's physical protection. A professor of a Christian college was watching the television one day and saw that an airplane leaving Miami had crashed into the Everglades. His son was supposed to fly out of Miami that day, so he checked the itinerary and saw that his son and a friend were scheduled to be on that plane. The professor called his wife, and they began to pray.

Two hours later he found out that his son and his friend had checked their bags, got their boarding passes and gone to the gate, but when it was time to board, the Holy Spirit spoke strongly to them, "Danger! Danger!"

They pulled back and did not board the plane, to the confusion of the boarding agent. Then, just as the jet was pulling away, another couple came running up waving their boarding passes saying, "We have to get on that plane!" The agents moved the walkway back to the plane, opened the door, and let them in. Everyone on that flight was killed just moments later.

There is strength, security, and protection in the presence of the Lord.

Number Four: Gladness

We talked about this in the first chapter, and I want to add a few more comments here. In the Hebrew language, gladness means ecstasy, exceeding joy. Jesus said:

> **He that believeth on me, as the scripture hath said, out of his belly shall flow rivers of living water.**
>
> **—John 7:38 (KJV)**

Romans says:

> For the kingdom of God is not meat and drink; but righteousness, and peace, and joy in the Holy Ghost.
>
> —Romans 14:17 (KJV)

And in the next chapter of Romans:

> Now the God of hope fill you with all joy and peace in believing, that ye may abound in hope, through the power of the Holy Ghost.
>
> —Romans 15:13 (KJV)

King David discovered this amazing truth. He said to God:

> Thou wilt shew me the path of life: in thy presence is fullness of joy; at thy right hand *there are* pleasures for ever more.
>
> —Psalm 16:11 (KJV)

When was the last time you experienced ecstasy? Joy is a natural result of the glory, honor and strength God gives us. How could you not be glad when your treasures are in Heaven, when your future is secure, and you are financially cared for and people admire you?

A man went to a psychologist and said, "I am depressed, dejected, and gloomy." The psychologist said, "I went to the circus last night, and there was a clown there who made me laugh. I recommend you go watch his act." The man said, "I am that clown!"

In London a few years back, a thick fog settled over the city for days with no wind to blow it away. The first day the suicide rate went way up. The second day the suicides doubled. The third day the suicides tripled. People cannot stay under clouds of depression. London needed a wind to blow that fog away. The word for spirit is the same word for wind – *pneuma*. When we suffer under depression we need the Holy Spirit to blow that depression away.

Where do you get your joy? Movies? Romance novels? Gossipy conversations? Many people do, but all they get is counterfeit joy. There is a better way: God's presence. I believe there is going to be a great understanding of the presence of the Lord before He comes to judge this earth, and that will cause great joy among those who believe. It will be a world where many fret over the future, but those who abide in God's presence will display an astonishing, uncanny joy.

Recently a man was telling me about a major revival and what people were experiencing there, and as he spoke I could only think, "Yes! That is what this church and every church needs." Moments later, after the man left, a flood of sheer ecstasy started flowing out of my belly. Something deep in my soul overflowed with joy so strong that I fell off my chair and laid on the floor letting it rush over me. I was glad nobody else was there!

The great revivalist of the nineteenth century, Charles Finney, had a similar experience when those "rivers of living water" Jesus spoke of began to flow into his soul. He wrote:

> "I returned to the front office, and found that the fire that I had made of large wood was nearly burned out. But as I turned and was about to take a seat by the fire, I received a mighty baptism of the Holy Ghost. Without any expectation of it, without ever having the thought in my mind that there was any such thing for me, without any recollection that I had ever heard the thing mentioned by any person in the world, the Holy Spirit descended upon me in a manner that seemed to go through body and soul. I could feel the impression, like a wave of electricity, going through and through me. Indeed it seemed to come in waves and waves of liquid love for I could not express it in any other way. It seemed like the very breath of God. I can recollect distinctly that it seemed to fan me, like immense wings.

> "No words can express the wonderful love that was shed abroad in my heart. I wept aloud with joy and love; and I do not know, but I should say, I literally bellowed out the unutterable gushings of my heart. These waves came over me, and over me, and over me, one after the other, until I recollect I cried out, 'I shall die if these waves continue

to pass over me.' I said, 'Lord, I cannot bear any more'; yet I had no fear of death." (Autobiography)[2]

Has such a thing ever happened to you? Beloved, you will know when it does! I cannot fully explain the theology of such things, but I know that "in His presence is fullness of joy," whether that means a sudden, dramatic experience or an ongoing, continuing gladness. Both are valid and welcome, and God knows when we need an extra dose of joy.

Seeing that these four important things — glory, honor, strength and gladness (and much more!) — are found in His presence, we need to ask, "How do we invite God's presence?" In the next chapter we will see one of the greatest ways to do that.

Chapter 3

Inviting God's Presence With Worship

God has a "wanted ad" in the personals. He is seeking someone who is compatible with Him, someone to spend time with Him, to love Him, to enjoy Him. He is so intent on finding this person that the Bible says His eyes go to and fro in the earth looking for someone who fits the description.

> For the eyes of the LORD run to and fro throughout the whole earth, to shew himself strong in the behalf of *them* whose heart *is* perfect toward him.
>
> **—2 Chronicles 16:9a (KJV)**

He is looking in every city in the world, on every continent, in every country. He has given the Holy Spirit an all-points bulletin to be on the lookout for him or her.

Who is the person God seeks? Does he have a particular name and address? Yes, and perhaps they are yours. What trait is He looking for in the person? Simply this:

This person must be a true worshiper.

Worship invites the presence of God in a way that perhaps nothing else can. Many people try so hard to please God in other ways when the real answer is simple. And yet only a small percentage of Christians learn this secret.

We define worship in so many different ways. For most of us, worship means the small slice of Sunday morning that we spend singing songs. I know, as does every Christian, that church services can get mechanical, with our inner clocks finely tuned to when worship starts, when we should stand up, how long the preacher should preach.

In a Pentecostal or Charismatic church service, worship begins when the slow songs start. We sing a fast chorus two or three times then flip the overhead to the next one. We sing that one, two, or three times, then flip up the next one, the songs get progressively slower. We watch the slide person put the wrong slide up, and we get distracted. When he finally gets it right, the song is over and we go to the next one, listen to someone in the choir sing in the wrong key and so forth until the song portion of the service ends. Then we sit down.

That is not worship!

No single experience, or church, can adequately define all that worship is. Scripture gives us a strong picture, though nowhere does it define it explicitly.

The fundamental meaning of worship is to ascribe worth to God.

Worship is not an event, but a lifestyle of ascribing worth to God, giving Him credit for who He is and what He does. From the time I wake up in the morning until the time I go to bed at night, and sometimes in the middle of the night, I remind myself to worship God because I want to remain in His presence. It is a magnificent way to live.

In John, chapter four, Jesus spoke to the woman at the well and said:

> Woman, believe me, the hour cometh, when ye shall neither in this mountain, nor yet at Jerusalem, worship the Father. Ye worship ye know not what: we know what we worship: for salvation is of the Jews. But the hour cometh, and now is, when the true worshippers shall worship the Father in spirit and in truth: for the Father seeketh such to worship Him.
>
> —John 4:21-23 (KJV)

Worship is an all-encompassing word, and underneath worship, as a subtitle, is praise. Psalm 100:4 says:

> **Enter his gates with thanksgiving and his courts with praise; give thanks to him and praise his name.**

Worship, which includes praise, brings us right into the presence of God, wherever we are.

Let's take a look at three words used for praise in the Bible — *hallel*, *yadah*, and *towdah*.

Hallel

This is the root word of hallelujah. Jah in the Hebrew language means Yahweh, or God. Hallel is to burst forth or boast in. Hallelujah means to burst forth with praise and boasting and bragging on Yahweh, or God or Jesus, to utterly enjoy to the fullest, to be proud of and to shout and rave over. It is being positively enthusiastic about the One in whom we are boasting. You might say it is going nuts over God. It defies respectability and demands emotional involvement. It takes us out of the fantasy world of religion and brings us into the presence of a real God.

Hallel demands a physical response.

- A bowing down of the body,
- A lifting up of the hands,

- A whirling around.

The house of God should be filled with laughter, movement, joy, and dancing! Psalm 100:1 says:

> Shout for joy to the LORD, all the earth.

Tambourines, maracas, raised voices and hand clapping are all fair game.

Psalm 100:2b (KJV) says:

> ...come before His presence with singing.

We ought to sing at the top of our lungs, lift our voices. It does not matter if you can carry a tune. What is noise to you is music in God's ears. I have been accused of singing in the key of Z, but it brings pleasure to the Father!

> I will praise *thee*, O LORD, with my whole heart; I will shew forth all thy marvellous works. I will be glad and rejoice in thee: I will sing praise to thy name, O thou most High.
>
> —Psalm 9:1-2 (KJV)

That's *hallel!* Worshiping with reckless abandon invites the presence of God.

Yadah

This means thanking the Lord for who He is.

> O give thanks unto the LORD; for *He* is good; for His mercy *endureth* for ever.
>
> —1 Chronicles 16:34 (KJV)

> Let us come before His presence with thanks-
> giving...
>
> —Psalm 95:2a (KJV)

In 2 Chronicles, we see what Hezekiah did after restoring honor to the temple.

> And Hezekiah appointed the courses of the
> priests and the Levites after their courses, every
> man according to his service, the priests and
> Levites for burnt offerings and for peace offer-
> ings, to minister, *and to give thanks,* and to praise
> in the gates of the tents of the LORD.
>
> —2 Chronicles 31:2 (KJV, italics added)

> Sing unto the LORD, O ye saints of His, and
> give thanks at the rememberance of His holi-
> ness.
>
> —Psalm 30:4 (KJV)

> *It is* a good *thing* to give thanks unto the LORD,
> and to sing praises unto thy name, O most High.
>
> —Psalm 92:1 (KJV)

It is good for us to give thanks to God for who He is, not just for what He does. It is selfless thanking. We learn to appreciate Him and His character apart from how it affects us. That will breed a thankful-ness of spirit in us toward God and toward our broth-ers and sisters that is not tied to what they can give us.

Towdah

This means to thank and praise Him for what He will do.

I preached at a church one time, and a couple of months later, a woman came to our church and said, "I am sure you do not know me, but I was over at that church you spoke at on Thanksgiving, and I was so depressed. The doctor told me I had cancer and there was nothing I could do. I was home moaning and groaning, and do not know what brought me to that service. But you started talking about Thanksgiving. I went home and started listing all the things to be thankful for. I started thanking my Jesus for all the great things He had done in my life and for the things He was going to do in the future. My appetite came back. Brother Dave, when I went back to the doctor, I found out there was no cancer in my body."

That woman practiced *towdah* — she thanked God in advance for what He would do.

Anna the prophetess thanked God for the baby Jesus long before Jesus began His ministry.

> **Coming up to them at that very moment, she gave thanks to God and spoke about the child to all who were looking forward to the redemption of Jerusalem.**
>
> **—Luke 2:38**

Jesus thanked God in advance many times. Before He fed the multitudes, He thanked God for the miracle that was about to occur (Matthew 14:19).

Before He served the first communion to His disciples, He gave thanks:

> **While they were eating, Jesus took bread, gave thanks and broke it, and gave it to his disciples, saying "Take and eat; this is my body." Then he took the cup, gave thanks and offered it to them saying, "Drink from it, all of you. This is my blood of the covenant which is poured out for many for the forgiveness of sins."**
>
> **—Matthew 26:26-28**

Jesus had not yet given His body to be broken or spilled His blood, but He thanked God in advance for what was about to happen at the cross. Thanking God before He does something is a form of praise and worship because it ascribes to Him power and might.

Learn By Doing

You do not learn praise and worship by reading about them but by doing them! It happens the same way you learn to play the piano. You have to sit down on that bench and put your fingers on the keys.

Go ahead! Make a joyful noise unto the Lord!

Many Christians do not want to worship or praise in the biblical manner. I remember watching a Christian television program where the hosts would declare the miracles of God, how He is alive today, and how we should celebrate Him with joy. Immediately following that was a rather dull-looking program on which the hosts would say exactly the opposite — how praise and music in the church was abolished in the New Testament.

Where did they get the idea that God did away with Old Testament praise? God has given us a progressive revelation, one that builds on what came before. Why would He abolish praise and worship now?

Those kinds of theories are attractive because some people are too prideful to worship in the biblical way. They are too proud to lift their hands, to participate in wild, reckless worship, whirling around, dancing, jumping up and down, shouting.

The first time I went to Calvary Chapel in the early 1970s and saw people lifting their hands up, I thought, "What in the world is going on in this place?" We sang a song, "Thy loving kindness is better than life, I lift my hands up," and everybody lifted their hands up, and so I lifted my hands up — not my arms, just my hands. I was controlled by the spirit of fear. After a while, I lifted my hands and elbows, and before the whole thing was said and done, I had both hands in the air. It took a few steps, but I got there.

True praise will always draw attention to the object of praise, not the praiser. For example, if you are the only one shouting, you are drawing attention to yourself, not to God. There has to be sensitivity.

There is also such a thing as false praise. I heard a preacher preaching against Catholics who use vain repetitions, and then he stepped back from the pulpit and said, "Hallelujah, hallelujah, hallelujah." If that was not vain repetition, I do not know what is! He figured a few hallelujahs on the end of his sentence might add credibility. That is not worshiping in spirit and in truth.

People everywhere are tired of religion, philosophy, and empty psychology. People want and need an experience with the living God, and when we *hallel,* and *yadah,* and *towdah* as a form of praise and worship, it brings the presence of Jehovah, or Yahweh, into the place. We have an encounter with God. True praising people and churches will see apostolic results. Without worship and praise, we will never find God's presence.

Practice a lifestyle of worship, ascribing worth to God at every opportunity and from the heart. In the next chapter, I will show you *Who* helps us.

Chapter 4

The Presence Is A Person

The presence of God is not just a "what" but a "Who." He is the Holy Spirit. If we are to worship in spirit and truth, and have the glory, honor, strength and gladness of living in God's presence, we must learn who this Person is and how to walk in a fourth-dimensional relationship with Him.

You see, humans were made to live in harmony with the Spirit of God and to have what people nowadays call a spiritual life. That means living in another dimension outside of our feelings and senses. It means being spiritually minded, not basing our lives on, "What do I feel? What do I see? What do I hear? How does this situation look?" but rather, "What does the Holy Spirit say?"

Merely being a "spiritual person," as is becoming more popular, does not necessarily mean a person has the presence of God. It may mean something quite different — that they have demons! Witches and mediums and New Age practitioners may have lively spiritual lives and may carry a supernatural presence with them, but it is not the presence of God, and sooner or later it will destroy them.

The Holy Spirit is the only one who can bring us the presence of God. In business terms, He is the sole distributor, copyright-holder, and owner of a God-ordained monopoly. He owns the universal rights to God's presence! And yet so many Christians neglect this Third Person of the Holy Trinity.

Pentecostal and Charismatic people often do not know the Holy Spirit any more than their mainline brethren. They know *about* the Holy Spirit — the gifts and power He brings. We talk about "waves of the Holy Spirit", "moves of the Holy Spirit." We are always praying for the Holy Spirit to do something. But precious few Pentecostals really *know* the Holy Spirit.

I would liken it to the relationship a man and woman have when they meet, court, and finally marry. At first they may think they know each other, and they do at some level. They enjoy the feelings they get by being together, and gradually they develop emotional intimacy. But when they come together on the wedding night that is a different kind of knowing! There is a big difference between knowing a person in the living room and knowing that person in the bedroom.

Do we know the Holy Spirit intimately? Have we cultivated a close relationship, or merely appreciated His power from afar?

Jesus said to His disciples:

> **And I will pray the Father, and He shall give you another Comforter, that He may abide with you for ever;**
>
> ***Even*** **the Spirit of truth; whom the world cannot receive, because it seeth Him not, neither knoweth Him: but ye know Him; for he dwelleth with you, and shall be in you.**
>
> **—John 14:16-17 (KJV)**

If you lack the presence of God in your life, it may be that you do not really know the Holy Spirit. You can go to every course on wisdom in the world and never come out a bit wiser unless the Spirit of wisdom has breathed into your life.

A little girl was composing a paper about electricity and wrote a letter to the power company that read:

> Dear sirs at the power company:
>
> I am 8 years old, and I am studying electricity for my class. Could you send me brochures you have on the subject of electricity? And if it is not too

much trouble, could you send me a sample of electricity? Thank you.

Like that little girl, many Christians are looking for a sample of the Holy Spirit. But a person cannot get a sample of the Holy Spirit any more than you can get a sample of electricity. We must launch into the deep, plug in to the main power source, make a decision, cross the line, and He will come to us.

Four Relationships With The Holy Spirit

There are four relationships a person can have with the Holy Spirit.

First, He is *with* us. This applies to people who do not know Christ. He is with the unsaved loved one whom you have been praying for. The Holy Spirit follows him into the tavern and convicts him of sin. As soon as that person starts drinking his beer, he feels empty. He does not know why, but it is because the Holy Spirit is with him at that moment. The presence of God is spoiling his "good time"!

Second, the Holy Spirit is *in* us as believers. When you and I turned from our sin, confessed and believed in Jesus Christ, the Holy Spirit came into our hearts. Every believer has the Holy Spirit in this way.

Third, He comes *upon* us. Jesus said, "And after that the Holy Spirit is come upon you," *(hepe*, a different Greek word,) "you shall receive power to be witnesses (Acts 1:8)." He is *in* every believer, but He is *upon* some believers. This means totally immersed, baptized in the Holy Spirit!

Then there is the fourth relationship, which I call the fourth-dimensional relationship. I knew about the first three relationships for twenty years before I discovered this often-overlooked fourth. It comes from the Greek word for comforter, *paracletes*, which means "a person who comes alongside to help, encourage, comfort, and give strength." In this fourth-dimensional relationship with the Holy Spirit, we allow Him to come along side of us, guide us, speak to us, literally tell us what to do and where to go. It is like He is with us, but it is more than that. It means an active, moment-by-moment inner conversation with God Himself.

When we walk in this fourth-dimensional relationship, we know a presence of God that is not available any other way. But this kind of relationship requires a certain atmosphere that we must develop and maintain. In the next chapter, I will tell you how.

"God loves to be with people who are sincere in their desire to follow Christ."

Chapter 5

The Atmosphere Of God

Living creatures have habitats. Mary Jo and I were in the Everglades riding on an airboat, and we saw alligators among the reeds. That is their habitat. You do not find them near my house in Michigan.

Humans can survive on earth, but not on the moon (without special equipment).

The Holy Spirit has a "habitat" too. He dwells in certain places and leaves others alone, and we actually have a say in whether or not He dwells in our life, our workplace, our church, or our campus.

I was talking with the Dean of Women at a Bible college, and she said the president was always speaking negatively: "We don't have this or that. Things are so messed up around here." A gloominess had settled over the campus. The Dean of Men committed suicide, a student committed suicide, and seven other students attempted it — all in one school year.

This friend of mine scheduled a meeting with the president and said, "Mr. President, do you know that the words of your mouth carry the power of life and death? When I came here, the first thing you said to me was, 'I cannot wait until some juicy situation happens that makes you squirm.' That offended me. Now we are in a juicy situation with suicides taking place on our campus, and yes, I am squirming, because that was one of my girls who died. All you do is talk negatively about the school. Why don't you start speaking life into this campus? Give thanks for what God has given us instead of complaining. If I have overstepped my bounds, my bags are packed and I am ready to go."

The presence of God was not on that campus. When people are involved in evil and wickedness, it creates a toxic atmosphere that drives out His active presence.

Inviting His Presence

What is the atmosphere that God loves? Worship and praise are part of it, as we saw earlier. Thankfulness and the other Fruits of the Spirit are part of it as well, but there is more, and here is what I have learned:

He loves to come into an atmosphere where He is not being offended.

What offends Him?

- Carelessness

- Laziness

- Unforgiveness

- Lack of reverence

- Worldly mindedness

The list goes on. Common sense tells us some of the things that drive Him away.

What drives *you* away? Rudeness? Gossip? Anger? Each of us has certain things that make us run away from a person or environment.

I love to give access to my life to people who do not offend me, who are careful to be concerned about what is important to me, who know my faults, yet do not try to change me. They let the Holy Spirit do His work.

But there are certain people to whom I cannot give access to my life because they are constantly gossiping about somebody else, or tearing somebody down, or bringing gloom to a situation, or speaking negatively. I am sure you know the same kinds of people.

They poison a room with their presence, and literally drive away the active presence of the Holy Spirit.

One man gave me a list of everything wrong with the church and my staff, and then said, "God has called me to be your personal assistant." I felt like telling him, "Take the garbage out, and hop in the dumpster yourself."

I think the Holy Spirit feels the same way sometimes, though He will not tell us to jump in a dumpster.

There are examples in the Bible of God leaving people or places. In Ezekiel, chapter 10, He removed His glory from the temple.

> **Then the glory of the LORD departed from over the threshold of the temple and stopped above the cherubim.**
>
> **—Ezekiel 10:18**

In the New Testament, Jesus was sometimes driven from a town, and He declared those places to be cursed.

> **Woe to you, Korazin! Woe to you, Bethsaida! If the miracles that were performed in you had been performed in Tyre and Sidon, they would have repented long ago in sackcloth and ashes. But I tell you, it will be more bearable for Tyre and Sidon on the day of judgment than for you.**
>
> **—Matthew 11:21-22**

It is sobering to think of God departing from us or cursing us like that, but if the atmosphere is not godly, and the people refuse to change, that is exactly what happens.

> **Let no corrupt communication proceed out of your mouth, but that which is good to the use of edifying, that it may minister grace unto the hearers. And grieve not the Holy Spirit of God, whereby ye are sealed unto the day of redemption.**
>
> **—Ephesians 4:29,30 (KJV)**

Cultivating The Right Atmosphere

How do we create the kind of atmosphere God loves? Here are some ideas:

• *Honor Him.* Don't treat godly things as common or mundane. Give Him the respect due a king, for that is what He is. Have reverence in your workplace, your church, and your home.

• *Be sincere of heart.* God loves to be with people who are sincere in their desire to follow Christ. They make mistakes — just look at how many mistakes the twelve disciples made! — but their hearts are pliable. It is the insincere heart that draws His wrath.

• *Be quick to repent.* We all mess up from time to time, but taking our mistake to God, asking for forgiveness, and getting a clean slate is extremely important.

55

• *Grow in the fruit of the Spirit:* love, joy, peace, patience, kindness, goodness, faithfulness, gentleness, and self-control.

• *Share Christ with others.* Don't be a swamp where no water goes in or out. Be a river where the water runs fresh all the time.

As you grow in your relationship with God, you will discover other ways to please Him in addition to the ones I have listed here.

In the next chapter, we will look at one of the most incredible, exciting benefits of walking with, and in, the presence of the Holy Spirit.

Chapter 6

The Presence Of Revival

When the Holy Spirit brings God's presence to a church or person, it causes revival — a sovereign, unusual, often amazing time of visitation. Revival is when a whole body of believers experiences a special manifestation of God's presence at one time.

Believers and churches should live in a constant state of revival, refreshing and renewal. Churches should grow continuously. Believers should always be maturing. We should experience the supernatural regularly, whether in an anointed worship service, a healing service or prayer meeting.

But the Holy Spirit also brings special times of visitation. I remember when such a revival hit our church not long ago.

A leadership and worker rally was scheduled for Thursday night, and I was supposed to speak, but by late afternoon, I still did not know what to say, and I did not feel that the Lord had given me anything to say. I asked one of the other pastors to prepare a message instead.

Just before the end of the workday, my secretary was walking out of the office, and I was standing in the reception area, but the minute I stepped into the office, the power of God hit me like a lightning bolt and threw me back into the reception area, and I burst forth in unintelligible languages from deep in my belly. I do not know how or why it happened, but I went back to my office and the Holy Spirit began to speak to me about many wonderful things. I enjoyed the experience to the fullest and then prepared for the meeting that evening.

During the leadership meeting, I felt the Lord nudge me to anoint all the leaders with oil, something I had not done in a long time. I always let my elders anoint people, but this time the Lord let me know He wanted me to do it and that He would refresh them.

I never dreamed what would happen next. I figured going into the meeting that it would last an hour, and then we would go out to eat, like always. But as I began to anoint people with oil, they fell out dramatically under the power of God, one after another, and they appeared lifeless. I thought I might have killed my leaders!

Some of them could not stand up and felt that a great weight was on top of them. Others were laughing, and others did not speak for hours afterward because they were struck with an awe of God. On and on it went, a lovely atmosphere of the presence of God. Leaders were laid out like a battlefield re-enactment of the Civil War, and when I finally looked at my watch I discovered that it was eleven o'clock— three hours after the meeting officially ended! It felt like only a few minutes had passed.

I am usually very uncomfortable with demonstrations like that. I want things in order, and I never want anyone to think we are a bunch of crazy people. The problem is, I usually put God in a box. The Gospels have so much weird stuff in them that would probably turn us off if it happened in church.

That night turned out to be the start of a wonderful season of revival at Mount Hope Church. Young people began to be radically involved in prayer and intercession, joining with the older saints who had been "radicalized" in revivals decades earlier.

Unsaved people began coming out of the woodwork, dropping by the church offices mid-week and asking how to get right with God!

And unusual things began happening that could only mean the Holy Spirit was bringing many people into a fourth-dimensional relationship with Him. One day shortly after the leadership meeting, one of the secretaries in our office was crying because she had been on vacation and missed the meeting. She had always prayed that when God poured out His Spirit in an unsually glorious way, she would be part of it. We decided to pray then and there for God to give her a fresh anointing of His Spirit, and as we did, a prophetic word came to me for her, and I began to speak it out as the Holy Spirit was giving it to me.

At the right moment, I put some oil on my hand and touched her, and she went out under the power of God. At about that time, my son roller-bladed down to the office with his friends. He said, "Hi, Dad," then noticed the secretary lying in the hall and leaned over and said, "What's happening?" I said, "God is visiting the office wing of Mount Hope Church." He said, "Cool," turned around and skated off!

We began attracting a crowd. Another secretary came out of her office, and we decided to pray for her, and she went down too. Another secretary came in to receive prayer and because she was pregnant we sat her in a chair so she would not hit the floor!

It was as though the presence of God was spreading through that place. There was such joy! People were laughing, overflowing with happiness and having a difficult time answering the phones with a straight face.

History In His Presence

That kind of thing has happened throughout history when God has decided to give people, churches, and countries an outpouring of His presence. Jonathan Edwards was a New England preacher in the 1700s when God visited America in a powerful way. We now know that event as the First Great Awakening. Before the revival, Edwards observed, sin ran rampant in his town. Young people stayed out late in mixed company; the taverns were busy, but church was considered drudgery. All of that changed.

> "This work of God soon made a glorious alteration in the town: so that in the spring and summer following, anno 1735, the town seemed to be full of the presence of God: it never was so full of love, nor of joy… the doings of God were then seen in His sanctuary, God's day was a delight, and His tabernacles were amiable. Our public assemblies were then beautiful: the congregation was alive in God's service, every one earnestly intent on the public worship, every hearer eager to drink in the words of the minister as they came from his

mouth; the assembly in general were, from time to time, in tears while the word was preached; some weeping with sorrow and distress, others with joy and love, others with pity and concern for the souls of their neighbors."

I love how he says the town was "full of the presence of God," full of love and joy, and that people wept during the preaching. He also said:

"Our public praises were then greatly enlivened; [people sang] with unusual elevation of heart and voice, which made the duty pleasant indeed... Those amongst us who had been formerly converted, were greatly enlivened, and renewed with fresh and extraordinary incomes of the Spirit of God.

"When once the Spirit of God began to be so wonderfully poured out in a general way through the town, people had soon done with their old quarrels, backbitings, and intermeddling with other men's matters. The tavern was soon left empty, and persons kept very much at home; none went abroad unless on necessary business, or on some religious account, and every day seemed in many respects, a Sabbath-day. ...The minister's house was thronged far more than ever the tavern had been." (Narrative of the Surprising Work of God)[3]

More than a century later, America was hit with another great awakening, this one led by Charles

Finney. He wrote of a time when he was preaching and:

> "In a few moments there seemed to fall upon the congregation an instantaneous shock. I cannot describe the sensation that I felt, nor that which was apparent in the congregation; but the word seemed literally to cut like a sword. The power from on high came down upon them in such a torrent that they fell from their seats in every direction. In less than a minute nearly the whole congregation were either down on their knees, or on their faces, or in some position prostrate before God. Everyone was crying or groaning for mercy upon his own soul. They paid no further attention to me or to my preaching." (Power From on High)[2]

The presence of God made them forget the preacher! That is the kind of experience people crave — divine visitation. As a preacher, I know full-well that I am helpless without the Holy Spirit. When I preach and do not get to all my notes, I hear the Holy Spirit say, "It will be all right. Leave the rest to me." I trust Him to do the work I could never do.

I have discovered that I have one person to make happy, and that is the Holy Spirit who has come along side to help me. I do not have to worry about impressing anybody or convicting anyone of sin. The Holy Spirit does it. When I try to do His job, I feel a strange emptiness in my belly.

If the Holy Spirit is not present in a church service, nothing significant will happen. We would be like priests in Ezekiel's day, when the glory of God left the temple. The priests still went about their duties. "Church" went on, but God's presence had left.

The apostle Paul was criticized for not being a good orator, and he responded by saying:

> And my speech and my preaching *was* not with enticing words of man's wisdom, but in demonstration of the Spirit and of power: That your faith should not stand in the wisdom of men, but in the power of God.
>
> —1 Corinthians 2:4-5 (KJV)

The Holy Spirit brings a demonstration of the power of God. There is no substitute.

One morning during the World Cup sailing race, the teams, camera crews, and officials woke up to start the race and discovered there was no wind, so the race had to be postponed.

When there is no wind, there is no race.

When there is no presence of the Holy Spirit, there is no ministry.

The same is true of us as individuals. If we do not have the Holy Spirit-born presence of God, nothing we do will matter. All the day-to-day struggles will be for naught. But if we have His presence, even the most menial things will be infused with meaning, joy, and thanksgiving.

I believe we are in the beginning stages of the last revival before Jesus comes. It is going to get to the point where it is unpopular *not* to be a Christian. God's presence will be more abundant than we have ever seen.

Are you ready for it? Are you comfortable in the presence of God? Are you accustomed to walking in a fourth-dimensional relationship with the Holy Spirit, letting Him lead and guide? If not, now is the time to get prepared!

"Every step away from sin takes us a step further into the presence of God."

Chapter 7

Walking In The Presence Of God

We have looked at four things that the presence of God brings: glory, honor, gladness, and strength. We have seen how worship invites the presence of God and how revival is the result.

The Bible lists other things that happen when we get into the presence of God. As you learn to walk in the presence of God, with the *paraclete* of the Holy Spirit beside you, you will begin to experience these wonderful benefits.

You Will Be Convicted Of Sin

You might think, "Some benefit!" In John 16:8 (KJV, brackets added), Jesus said:

> And when He [the Holy Spirit] is come, He will reprove the world of sin, and of righteousness and, of judgment.

The Holy Spirit and the presence of God reprove us, and for our own good. It does not say He will *accuse* the world of sin, but reprove, which means He will reveal sin in all its ugliness…and give us a way out. God never points the finger at our sin without also pointing to the exit door from where we can escape.

Every step away from sin takes us a step further into the presence of God. As you cultivate that fourth-dimensional relationship, you will notice that God points to more things He wants removed from your life: petty lying, worry, overwork, anger — whatever conflicts with His character. When David was reproved of sin, he prayed, "O, Lord, take not Thy Holy Spirit from me." He was desperate not to lose the presence of God.

Your Mortal Body Will Be Quickened

Paul wrote:

> And if the Spirit of him who raised Jesus from the dead is living in you, he who raised Christ from the dead will also give life to your mortal bodies through his Spirit, who lives in you.
>
> —Romans 8:11

I used to think that meant that on the day of resurrection my body would come out of the grave. Then I re-read it and saw that it meant our mortal bodies — the ones we are in right now. The presence of God "vitalizes" our bodies, giving us more energy than we would naturally have.

The great woman of the Spirit, Kathryn Kuhlman, would pray for three hours before each service, walking back and forth in high heels behind the stage. During the four- and five-hour services, she would stand the whole time, then go backstage to meet local dignitaries and ministers. Someone who worked with her asked how she did it and she replied, "Romans 8 says the same Spirit that raised Jesus from the dead will quicken your mortal body. If you see it in God's Word, you can have it."

Some people complain of lethargy, but people walking in God's presence will have energy to spare.

You Will See Truth Clearly

On the night He was betrayed, Jesus told the disciples:

> But when He, the Spirit of truth, comes, He will guide you into all truth. He will not speak on His own; He will speak only what He hears, and he will tell you what is yet to come. He will bring glory to me by taking from what is mine and making it known to you.
>
> —John 16:13-14

Jesus called the Holy Spirit the Spirit of Truth. Jesus Himself is the Truth, and the Holy Spirit leads us into a deeper relationship with Jesus.

The more you walk with the Holy Spirit, the more clearly you will see the truth. Like Solomon, you will have wisdom beyond your training or natural abilities.

- You will see people's motives.

- You will recognize the wise path in difficult circumstances.

- You will give good counsel to friends.

The Holy Spirit gives daily, incremental enlightenment.

You Will Be Adopted

> For ye have not received the spirit of bondage again to fear, but ye have received the Spirit of adoption, whereby we cry, Abba, Father. The Spirit itself beareth witness with our spirit, that we are the children of God.
>
> —Romans 8:15-16 (KJV)

When you believe in Christ, the Creator of everything becomes your Daddy ("Abba Father").

The Holy Spirit baptizes us into Christ and adopts us into God's family. We no longer have a religious, stilted, formal relationship with God. We can crawl into the Father's lap and ask Him for anything.

The further you go into the Presence, the more comfortable and relational you will be with Father God.

> **The Spirit Himself testifies with our spirit that we are God's children.**
>
> —**Romans 8:16**

As you understand that you are a child of God, your self-image goes up. You understand you are part of a good family.

> **If ye then, being evil, know how to give good gifts unto your children, how much more shall your Father which is in heaven give good things to them that ask Him?**
>
> —**Matthew 7:11 (KJV)**

You Will Receive Revelation Knowledge

Revelation knowledge is knowledge that pops into our hearts that we would not know unless the Holy Spirit revealed it to us.

Jesus had a constant stream of revelation knowledge and knew people's hearts, histories, and motives before they spoke — and even before He met them.

• He told the woman at the well about her checkered past (John 4:16-18).

• He predicted that the disciples would abandon Him (Matthew 26:31).

• He constantly peered into the hearts of the Scribes and Pharisees and told them what wickedness He saw.

In the book of Acts, the Holy Spirit gave revelation knowledge to Christians as they needed it:

• Peter knew supernaturally that Ananias and Sapphira had lied about the amount of money they brought to the apostles (Acts 5:1-11).

• Paul learned in a dream that his boat would shipwreck, but that no lives would be lost (Acts 27).

• Philip received instructions to go to Ethiopia, and on the way met and converted a high government official (Acts 8:26-40).

Dozens, even hundreds, of times in the Bible we find the Holy Spirit dropping bits of revelation into people's hearts.

It happens today too. I can't count the number of times the Holy Spirit has given me just the right bit of knowledge at the right time and for the right purpose. He doesn't do it to be spooky, but to accomplish some purpose:

- salvation

- healing

- conviction

- comfort

- wisdom

Paul wrote:

> **The Spirit searches all things, even the deep things of God. For who among men knows the thoughts of a man except the man's spirit within him? In the same way no one knows the thoughts of God except the Spirit of God. We have not received the spirit of the world but the Spirit who is from God, that we may understand what God has freely given us.**
>
> **—1 Corinthians 2:10b-12**

You will find this happening to you too. While you are talking to a friend, the Holy Spirit may drop a sliver of knowledge into your mind, and when you speak it, it brings clarity to the situation or lays the person's heart bare.

Or you may simply hear the voice of the Holy Spirit telling you not to take a certain route home, and you find out later that there was a terrible accident that you could have been involved in. Giving you the right revelation at the right time is part of His job.

There are a lot of smart people who are going to hell. Some of the smartest scientists, novelists, politicians, and geniuses are going to hell because they do not have spiritual understanding, thus refuse to come to Jesus Christ.

You Will Change From One Glory To Another

Paul wrote:

> And we, who with unveiled faces all reflect the Lord's glory, are being transformed into his likeness with ever-increasing glory, which comes from the Lord, who is the Spirit.
>
> —2 Corinthians 3:18

One of the most freeing things I have ever learned is that I cannot change myself. I have to fall on the grace of God, and the work of Christ on the cross, and the power of the Holy Spirit to perform a work in my life, and then the changes come.

You can hold your breath, stand on your head, bribe, strive, connive, but the change will not come until it is Spirit-led.

You ought not say, "I am going to change," but, "Holy Spirit, I am going to follow Your leading."

Then you will notice the remarkable, subtle but powerful fact: God is changing you from the inside out. Hallelujah!

Last Word

Isn't it wonderful to know that God shares His presence with us? Now let me give you a point-by-point plan to help you cultivate, activate and invite the presence of God into your life:

• **Seek the presence of God.** We learned that though God is everywhere, not everybody shares His power and presence, and many people never experience it even once. Press into Him. Make it your life's goal to live in His presence day in and day out.

• **Rely on God's presence for your happiness.** Anything else will disappoint.

• **Spend time at church.** Absorb the presence of God that is present when you meet with other believers. Remember, ten seconds in His presence can do more than a lifetime of striving.

• **Rejoice!** Consider how blessed you are to share in God's presence.

• **Invite His presence with worship**. Become a true worshiper. Dance, sing, shout, be emotional, and thank Him for who He is, what He has done and what He is going to do.

• **Get to know the Holy Spirit.** He brings the presence of God and does more for us than we could ever think to ask for.

• **Cultivate an atmosphere that invites the Holy Spirit.** Speak positively, don't gossip, have reverence, be sincere, desire the Lord, repent quickly, cultivate the fruit of the Spirit in your life, and you will create a place where God loves to dwell.

• **Spend time alone with the Holy Spirit.** Just as married couples need face-to-face time, we need it with the Holy Spirit too. It will foster great intimacy with Him.

• **Pray for revival.** Every individual and church needs times of refreshing. Start or join a prayer meeting where you pray for revival to visit your city.

This simple summary will help you remember the powerful truths we have discussed in this book. I pray that the power and presence of God would daily increase in your life, making you an even mightier man or woman of God.

End Notes:

Chapters One and Two:
1.) The Practice of the Presence of God, Conversations and Letters of Brother Lawarence, public domain
2.) Power From On High, Charles G. Finney, public domain

Chapter Six:
2.) Power From On High, Charles G. Finney, public domain
3.) A Faithful Narrative of the Surprising Work of God, Jonathan Edwards, public domain.

About The Author

Dave Williams is pastor of Mount Hope Church and International Outreach Ministries, with world headquarters in Lansing, Michigan. He has served for over 20 years, leading the church in Lansing from 226 to over 4000 today. Dave sends trained ministers into unreached cities to establish disciple-making churches, and, as a result, today has "branch" churches in the United States, Philippines, and in Africa.

Dave is the founder and president of Mount Hope Bible Training Institute, a fully accredited institute for training ministers and lay people for the work of the ministry. He has authored 55 books including the fifteen-time best seller, *The New Life...The Start of Something Wonderful* (with over 2,000,000 books sold), and more recently, *The Miracle Results of Fasting, The Road To Radical Riches,* and *Angels.*

The Pacesetter's Path telecast is Dave's weekly television program seen over a syndicated network of secular stations, and nationally over the Sky Angel satellite system. Dave has produced over 125 audio cassette programs including the nationally acclaimed *School of Pacesetting Leadership* which is being used as a training program in churches around the United States, and in Bible Schools in South Africa and the Philippines. He is a popular speaker at conferences, seminars, and conventions. His speaking ministry has taken him across America, Africa, Europe, Asia, and other parts of the world.

Along with his wife, Mary Jo, Dave established The Dave and Mary Jo Williams Charitable Mission (Strategic Global Mission), a mission's ministry for providing scholarships to pioneer pastors and grants to inner-city children's ministries.

Dave's articles and reviews have appeared in national magazines such as *Advance, The Pentecostal Evangel, Ministries Today, The Lansing Magazine, The Detroit Free Press* and others. Dave, as a private pilot, flies for fun. He is married, has two grown children, and lives in Delta Township, Michigan.

You may write to Pastor Dave Williams:

P.O. Box 80825

Lansing, MI 48908-0825

Please include your special prayer requests when you write, or you may call the Mount Hope Global Prayer Center: (517) 327-PRAY

DECAPOLIS
PUBLISHING

For a catalog of products, call:

1-517-321-2780 or

1-800-888-7284

or visit us on the web at:

www.mounthopechurch.org

For Your Spiritual Growth

Here's the help you need for your spiritual journey. These books will encourage you, and give you guidance as you seek to draw close to Jesus and learn of Him. Prepare yourself for fantastic growth!

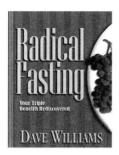

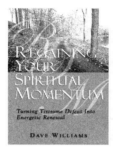

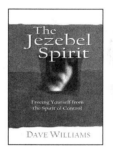

RADICAL FASTING
How would you like to achieve your dreams at "break-neck" speed? Radical fasting may be your key!

REGAINING YOUR SPIRITUAL MOMENTUM
Use this remarkable book as your personal street map to regain your spiritual momentum.

THE JEZEBEL SPIRIT
Do you feel controlled? Learn more about what the Bible says about this manipulating principality's influence.

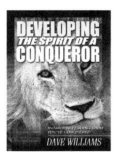

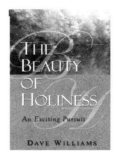

DEVELOPING THE SPIRIT OF A CONQUEROR
Take back what the enemy has stolen from you. Learn how to engage your authority and *Develop the Spirit of a Conqueror.*

BEAUTY OF HOLINESS
We face the choice — holiness or rebellion. True holiness comes about by working together in cooperation with the Holy Spirit.

ABCs OF SUCCESS & HAPPINESS
God wants to give you every good gift, so it's time to accept the responsibility for your success today!

These and other books available from Dave Williams and:

DECAPOLIS
PUBLISHING

For Your Spiritual Growth

Here's the help you need for your spiritual journey. These books will encourage you, and give you
guidance as you seek to draw close to Jesus and learn
of Him. Prepare yourself for fantastic growth!

**QUESTIONS I HAVE
ANSWERED**
Get answers to many of
the questions you've
always wanted to ask a
pastor!

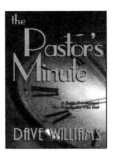

THE PASTOR'S MINUTE
A daily devotional for
people on the go!
Powerful topics will
help you grow even
when you're in a hurry.

**ANGELS: THEY ARE
WATCHING YOU!**
The Bible tells more than
you might think about these
powerful beings.

THE WORLD BEYOND
What will Heaven be like?
What happens there? Will
we see relatives who have
gone before us? Who
REALLY goes to Heaven?

FILLED!
Learn how you can be
filled with the mightiest
power in the universe.
Find out what could be
missing from your life.

**STRATEGIC GLOBAL
MISSION**
Read touching stories about
God's plan for accelerating
the Gospel globally
through reaching children
and training pastors.

**These and other books
available from Dave Williams and:**

DECAPOLIS
PUBLISHING

For Your Spiritual Growth

Here's the help you need for your spiritual journey. These books will encourage you, and give you guidance as you seek to draw close to Jesus and learn of Him. Prepare yourself for fantastic growth!

HOW TO BE A HIGH PERFORMANCE BELIEVER
Pour in the nine spiritual additives for real power in your Christian life.

SECRET OF POWER WITH GOD
Tap into the real power with God; the power of prayer. It will change your life!

THE NEW LIFE...
You can get off to a great start on your exciting life with Jesus! Prepare for something wonderful.

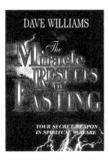

MIRACLE RESULTS OF FASTING
You can receive MIRACLE benefits, spiritually and physically, with this practical Christian discipline.

WHAT TO DO IF YOU MISS THE RAPTURE
If you miss the Rapture, there may still be hope, but you need to follow these clear survival tactics.

THE AIDS PLAGUE
Is there hope? Yes, but only Jesus can bring a total and lasting cure to AIDS.

These and other books available from Dave Williams and:

DECAPOLIS PUBLISHING

For Your Spiritual Growth

Here's the help you need for your spiritual journey. These books will encourage you, and give you guidance as you seek to draw close to Jesus and learn of Him. Prepare yourself for fantastic growth!

THE ART OF PACESETTING LEADERSHIP
You can become a successful leader with this proven leadership development course.

GIFTS THAT SHAPE YOUR LIFE
Learn which ministry best fits you, and discover your God-given personality gifts, as well as the gifts of others.

GROWING UP IN OUR FATHER'S FAMILY
You can have a family relationship with your heavenly father. Learn how God cares for you.

SUPERNATURAL SOULWINNING
How will we reach our family, friends, and neighbors in this short time before Christ's return?

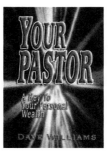

YOUR PASTOR: A KEY TO YOUR PERSONAL WEALTH
By honoring your pastor you can actually be setting yourself up for a financial blessing from God!

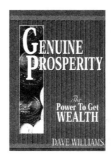

GENUINE PROSPERITY
Learn what it means to be truly prosperous! God gives us the power to get wealth!

These and other books available from Dave Williams and:

DECAPOLIS PUBLISHING

For Your Spiritual Growth

Here's the help you need for your spiritual journey. These books will encourage you, and give you guidance as you seek to draw close to Jesus and learn of Him. Prepare yourself for fantastic growth!

SOMEBODY OUT THERE NEEDS YOU
Along with the gift of salvation comes the great privilege of spreading the gospel of Jesus Christ.

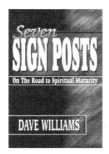

SEVEN SIGNPOSTS TO SPIRITUAL MATURITY
Examine your life to see where you are on the road to spiritual maturity.

THE PASTORS PAY
How much is your pastor worth? Who should set his pay? Discover the scriptural guidelines for paying your pastor.

DECEPTION, DELUSION & DESTRUCTION
Recognize spiritual deception and unmask spiritual blindness.

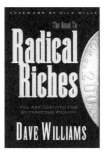

THE ROAD TO RADICAL RICHES
Are you ready to jump from "barely getting by" to Gods plan for putting you on the road to Radical Riches?

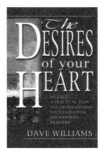

THE DESIRES OF YOUR HEART
Yes, Jesus wants to give you the desires of your heart, and make them realities.

For Your Successful Life

These video cassettes will give you successful principles to apply to your whole life. Each a different topic, and each a fantastic teaching of how living by God's Word can give you total success!

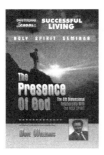

THE PRESENCE OF GOD
Find out how you can have a more dynamic relationship with the Holy Spirit.

FILLED WITH THE HOLY SPIRIT
You can rejoice and share with others in this wonderful experience of God.

GIFTS THAT CHANGE YOUR WORLD
Learn which ministry best fits you, and discover your God-given personality gifts, as well as the gifts of others.

THE SCHOOL OF PACESETTING LEADERSHIP
Leaders are made, not born. You can become a successful leader with this proven leadership development course.

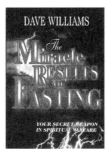

MIRACLE RESULTS OF FASTING
Fasting is your secret weapon in spiritual warfare. Learn how you'll benefit spiritually and physically! Six video messages.

A SPECIAL LADY
If you feel used and abused, this video will show you how you really are in the eyes of Jesus. You are special!

These and other videos available from Dave Williams and:

DECAPOLIS PUBLISHING

For Your Successful Life

These video cassettes will give you successful principles to apply to your whole life. Each a different topic, and each a fantastic teaching of how living by God's Word can give you total success!

HOW TO BE A HIGH PERFORMANCE BELIEVER
Pour in the nine spiritual additives for real power in your Christian life.

THE UGLY WORMS OF JUDGMENT
Recognizing the decay of judgment in your life is your first step back into God's fullness.

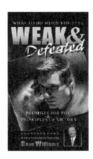

WHAT TO DO WHEN YOU FEEL WEAK AND DEFEATED
Learn about God's plan to bring you out of defeat and into His principles of victory!

WHY SOME ARE NOT HEALED
Discover the obstacles that hold people back from receiving their miracle and how God can help them receive the very best!

BREAKING THE POWER OF POVERTY
The principality of mammon will try to keep you in poverty. Put God FIRST and watch Him bring you into a wealthy place.

HERBS FOR HEALTH
A look at the concerns and fears of modern medicine. Learn the correct ways to open the doors to your healing.

These and other videos available from Dave Williams and:

DECAPOLIS PUBLISHING

Running Your Race

These simple but powerful audio cassette singles will help give you the edge you need. Run your race to win!

LONELY IN THE MIDST OF A CROWD
Loneliness is a devastating disease. Learn how to trust and count on others to help.

HERBS FOR HEALTH
A look at the concerns and fears of modern medicine. Learn the correct ways to open the doors to your healing.

HOW TO GET ANYTHING YOU WANT
You can learn the way to get anything you want from God!

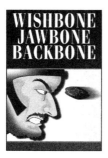

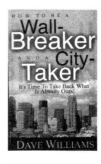

WISHBONE, JAWBONE, BACKBONE
Learn about King David, and how his three "bones" for success can help you in your life quest.

FATAL ENTICEMENTS
Learn how you can avoid the vice-like grip of sin and it's fatal enticements that hold people captive.

HOW TO BE A WALL BREAKER AND A CITY TAKER
You can be a powerful force for advancing the Kingdom of Jesus Christ!

These and other audio tapes available from Dave Williams and:

DECAPOLIS PUBLISHING

Expanding Your Faith

These exciting audio teaching series will help you to grow and mature in your walk with Christ. Get ready for amazing new adventures in faith!

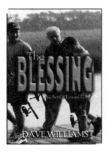

THE BLESSING
Explore the many ways that God can use you to bless others, and how He can correct the missed blessing.

SIN'S GRIP
Learn how you can avoid the vice-like grip of sin and it's fatal enticements that hold people captive.

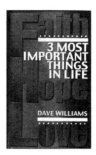

FAITH, HOPE, & LOVE
Listen and let these three "most important things in life" change you.

PSALM 91 THE PROMISE OF PROTECTION
Everyone is looking for protection in these perilous times. God promises protection for those who rest in Him.

DEVELOPING THE SPIRIT OF A CONQUEROR
You can be a conqueror through Christ! Also, find out how to *keep* those things that you have conquered.

WHY DO SOME SUFFER
Find out why some people seem to have suffering in their lives, and find out how to avoid it in your life.

These and other audio tapes available from Dave Williams and:

DECAPOLIS PUBLISHING

Expanding Your Faith

These exciting audio teaching series will help you to grow and mature in your walk with Christ. Get ready for amazing new adventures in faith!

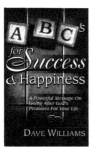

ABCs OF SUCCESS AND HAPPINESS
Learn how to go after God's promises for your life. Happiness and success can be yours today!

FORGIVENESS
The miracle remedy for many of life's problems is found in this basic key for living.

UNTANGLING YOUR TROUBLES
You can be a "trouble untangler" with the help of Jesus!

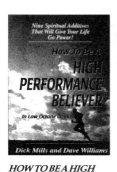

HOW TO BE A HIGH PERFORMANCE BELIEVER
Put in the nine spiritual additives to help run your race and get the prize!

BEING A DISCIPLE AND MAKING DISCIPLES
You can learn to be a "disciple maker" to almost anyone.

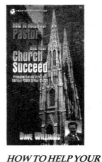

HOW TO HELP YOUR PASTOR & CHURCH SUCCEED
You can be an integral part of your church's & pastor's success.

These and other audio tapes available from Dave Williams and:

DECAPOLIS PUBLISHING